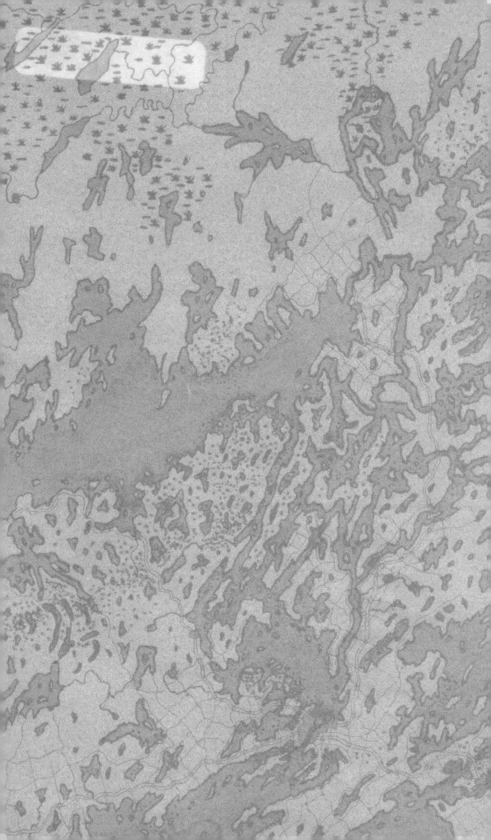

# Cartography
## and Walking

# Cartography
## and Walking

# Adam
# Dickinson

Brick Books

National Library of Canada Cataloguing in Publication Data

Dickinson, Adam, 1974-
    Cartography and walking

Poems.
ISBN 1-894078-22-5

I. Title

PS8557.I3235C37 2002     C811'.6     C2001-904092-X
PR9199.4.D52C37 2002

We gratefully acknowledge the Canada Council for the Arts,
the Government of Canada through the Book Publishing
Industry Development Program (BPIDP), and the Ontario
Arts Council for their support of our publishing programme.

The cover photograph is the work of Bruce Litteljohn.
The author photograph was taken by Dorothy Field.
The maps on the end paper and pages 10, 43 and 69
were drawn by the author and reproduced with the
help of Gabrielle Zezulka-Mailloux.

This book is set in Minion and Meta.

Design and layout by Alan Siu.

Printed and bound by Sunville Printco Inc.

Brick Books
431 Boler Road, Box 20081
London, Ontario   N6K 4G6

brick.books@sympatico.ca

This book is
for Mom, Dad,
and Kim.

# Table of Contents

## Part I: Escarpments

**Part II: Cordillera**

**Part III: Standing Water**

# Part I
# Escarpments

# Part I
# Escarpments

## Disappointment in the Masonry

There is little doubt
that bats are in the chimney.
At dusk, you can hear
the folded sheets
of their slender ascent,
a private appearance
over rooftops,
the steam from a bath
that has just been filled.

Their modesty confounds us.
They dart in the cover of tree tops
as though rushing from bathrooms to dress.
When we see them in the dark
we are half of the mind
they are leaves we've mistaken.

One evening, something
clung to the ceiling
above the fireplace,
cramped in its brown shiver,
the body of an old man
hunched before a tub.
We didn't think to get
the paddle or the broom,
but opened all of the windows,
turned out the lamps,
and felt for the railing to the street,
its cold abashment
working blindly in our hands.

## Or Was It the Smell of Cut Wood

The rain organizes itself on the pavement,
the clouds are burned towels draped
over the oven doors of buildings above
the grey, milling sidewalks of town.

Even as the forest keeps beyond the streets,
it does so as allowance, a concession
to the nerve it took to stand among these spruce,
among the black and brutal mallets of their heads.

When it rains the mill plumes belly over tree tops,
the overcast itself conveys the smell of cut wood;
a dangerous proposition: too little and the boreal
loses its fear, too strong and the conifers rally,

withdraw their concessions, plug the town with pitch,
emerge in the cleared grounds of parks and yards,
and swing their black bats about the oven doors
breaking union ranks with their granite trust.

## Having to Start the Garden Alone

How long has winter slouched in this garden?
Mornings I hack black rows
and they are dead musicians,
their instruments clotted at their mouths.
I go out with the sun to lay seeds
but the soil is a tap that has been running,
its cold is thick with slurred speech.
Once, we filled the yard with garden,
a great coral waving its limbs,
a brain lying open before us, its nerves
alive in our food. When you were buried,
I thought of pumpkin vines,
hands spread, feeling the surprise of dirt,
the wind enough that day to blow pollen
from the trees, a yellow mist,
a snow of ground mustard, falling.
I have let the muscle of garden weaken;
it crouches with the cold inside it like an anthem
for a country that is gone; it is frost
that bells within me now when I work.
As I water the rows,
your voice is the needles of high brass
that living things make when they freeze.

## Get the Kids to Bring in a Log of Black Cherry

Right before the dog died,
its dark eyes reached out
from in front of the woodpile
like two halves of a piece of split cherry.
The clean grain stared at us
from the back of the shed,
as though two pools of tea
had steeped there and held.

Once, we helped Dad cut a tree
whose canopy had become riddled.
Red soil spit from the middle
of each of the chainsaw cuts.
When we moved the logs, our hands
glistened with moist tannin
like soaking in a kettle drum
of rusted rain.

The dog had been sluggish for days,
wouldn't even eat the bacon fat
that had to be carried to the shed.
We never expected the eyes,
their smooth plates washed suddenly
at our faces in the doorway,
drawing warmth from our skin
like a room heated by a fire of green wood.

## Something Made Me Think of Bears

It could have been the honey
that sat in the back of the fridge.
The jar itself made my hands tacky
shifting it among the milks and fruits,
as though one were shearing the lower boughs
of pines, handling them quickly,
only noticing the pitch in the crease of a grip.

As a child, I grew up next door to a trapper.
He would emerge from the woods
with his clasps and claws, his smell,
the black bottom of an overturned stump.
In the weeks of his travel, we would sneak
through the vestibule window
to a tub of honey he kept beneath the sink.

He called on my father one evening,
after spending a month on the line.
You could see that the honey
was bright on his lips, made his words
smack together as though he needed a drink.
They walked past me to the kitchen,
my father took meat from the fridge.

## The Cardinal

The cardinal confirms your sense of injury,
dashed in the branches
like a fresh cut on a forearm.

It could be the bird is wounded,
damaged on the inside
to a slow bruising of blood through feathers.

In the beginning, it might have been an accident,
its early wings affixed with excessive force,
or perhaps a terrible wisdom

had impressed itself like a bald sun
after trees have been cut from the street,
and leaves have rusted in the drains.

You see the cardinal in this colour,
carrying the shimmer of its burst
in the startled space of its bones.

You recall yourself at one time
having had the blush of olives in your breast
before the red of indignation,

and then the tired heat of giving in
to the repair. You held the darkness here
and then rested.

In the end, the injury is overcast,
touched upon the branches and decisions,
flushed upon the lips of prayers, broken open.

## When We Stand, We Are Leaning

It could be that all construction eventually comes down to
      bridges.
With its planking pulled aside, the renovation
gives the church its bearing beams.
The bruise on your arm is a carefully poised suspension
tending to the tarnish of its capillaries.
Even in the words we use for sadness, there are bridges;
melancholy slumps into the fog like leaning rails;
dejection clicks and then continues past a river.

Yet, the summer we learned to canoe, it wasn't the brace
of the paddle and thwart, but the trick of ferrying that obsessed
      us,
the light pad of our hull sideways across rapids,
like a girl looking up while running, chewing gum with her
      mouth open.
We thought of the canoe as an airplane wing,
as a way of landing without remaining,
the moment the boughs of a spruce reach for a squirrel, and
      then slacken,
sparing the high and rigid rafters of always trying to touch.

## Into the Hooves of Horses

The wind picked up a few days earlier,
passed over the city like a frightened horse,
and today has moved off to the lake
where she can see it breathing and kicking.
On these days she thinks she sees him
in the house, his head bent taking the stairs,
the tap of his cane on the pine in the hall.
She had to reseal old cans in the basement,
some paint he had used for touching the trim.
He emerges from this kind of weather for her
like the bright flesh of squash flowers
that appear almost lost in the crosshatch of green
where the garden blows over the lip of the grass.
He occurs in the drapes that are whipped
by the gusts as they spread to a gallop and curl.
But today it has calmed everywhere around her,
except in the garden beneath the bedroom,
where the wind fills the raspberries and has set them
to chipping the paint. She can feel the breeze
turning in off the lake, she takes its hair in her hand.

## He Who Waits for Spring

You, from the bed,
as a leaf curls from a stem,
and I with my orchids underfed,
have placed a naked branch
to mind the absence of your head:
to grow again, to nourish,
and to have fled.

## Making Use of Franklin

It is perhaps a single bone somewhere
that guides the polar bear
to her denning site in autumn;
a throb at the back of her neck,
a give in her footstep
that she cannot correct.

Our maps direct us
to parts of ourselves.
We know of headlands near the harbour
that emerge from the spit,
the north arm of a lake
and the cape that stiffens behind it.

Sailors have crowded the arctic,
searched for the mouths
of Chinese rivers.
Their bones are splinters there
where the only wood washes
like blanched cartilage to shore.

Franklin held on to silverware
for runes to read in the cold.
His family crest was a compass
carved in the steel of each spoon,
pointing the way to open water,
a map so easily ruined.

## When We Become Desirable

There is a genus of spruce so enamoured with the sky
it is painful to look at its blue needles –
like watching someone give themselves
so wholly to a doomed love
that you know you can do little,
except be there when the crepuscular heart fails.
Its limbs are the blue under your nails, in your lips
when the cold has opened its umbrella inside you.
In winter, the shadows in its crown
are footprints through a playground in deep snow
collecting the bruised light of retreating children;
it takes some time to recover yourself
after seeing this in the late afternoon.
It is not the kind of tree you can climb,
but often its lower branches hang down
like the sloped walls of a tent you can enter
and be, for a moment, among the pitch and splinters
of wanting, with all the colour of your blue-veined blood,
what will not receive you.

## Portraits

There is, perhaps, the inkling of ruin
in a people that asks of its painters,
portraits.

By the bridges of shadow that divide
a nobleman's brow, the gravity
of government becomes more
than the gothic solemnity of buildings,
more than the careful writs reserved
on the shelves of a marshalling ministry.

With his back to the window, the water
in a painted child's eye is the burning of livestock,
the trembling of cannons at dusk.
His enfolded hands are a setting of china
in habits that have been misplaced.

Perhaps expedience craves the portrait.
If the cities returned to ruins,
the parliaments declined to rocks, and the language
of things became cracked and unspoken, a portrait
would offer a map of restoration.

The way the angles of lips impart the order
of an afternoon swim, the spectral
strength of a bishop, the compulsion
to shatter a place that lays such poverty
in a child's face.

When portraits are required of painters,
perhaps, there is the sense among a people
that something must survive them,
that something must come down to stand
for what was in the light.

## Both In and Out of Sight

There are moments
when wings are drawn out
by the brush of a twig,
or the narrative exposed
by the dip of a chin.
It is to these
that one must give in.

I am acting out the flood of cardinals,
ripened all day in the trees.
I return to you in unfurling waves,
at once deliberate
and seized.

# More Water, We Thought

The river gave up the dog at the end of the summer,
concerned itself instead with picking through the rocks,
foraging to fill ruts and troughs,
like rummaging through the underbrush for blueberries
to bake in the lid of a cast iron pot.
We too had to make do at the cottage,
sitting to dinner with only two spoons,
drinking tea from jam jars we found
and cleaned with handfuls of moss.

We had come again this weekend to look for the dog,
refill his dish where the squirrels had spilled
what we hoped would bring him home.
It was while eating, holding two sticks in the salad,
that you noticed the white flaw in the river,
the soft jacket that someone had let drop
from around a waist and balloon in its small, trapped lung.
It took both of us to pull him out, dinner grew cold,
the pie stuck to the bottom of the lid.

Searching is an arid business, a parched throat
on a day of no clouds. Once in Midland
we linked arms with swimmers and felt with our feet
for a boy who'd gone missing. He was thick in the water,
a piece of swollen bread, his skin the grey of timber wolves
who come down to the far shore of our river to drink.
We had to dig the dog's grave with our hands.
Our skin was split and our nails purple and red;
on the car ride home through the lakes
we ate handfuls of blueberries for something to drink.

## Looking at the Teeth of a Wet Saw

You could not forgive me,
as though I were wind
and had brought down trees,
as though I were the neighbourhood
near the site of a drowning
and had offered nothing,
as though I were the ration of water
in the concrete of the bridge
and had turned to rejoin the river.

You could not forgive the failure
in a robin's egg.
Its damp feathers unhinging in the dark,
collecting and swelling, but never breaking;
nor its presence in the birdsong,
as in your dream, the dead weight
of my tongue.

## Cedar Canvas

There is something in the way canoes come
from a carpenter's mind;
the weight of an acuity played out in the planing.
The emergence is monkish,
is already a thoroughly conceived community.
When the carpenter thinks, he is running through branches
back into the wood, reversing the carving,
moving as something both ripened and green.

When the ribs are steamed,
the wood is bent back again as a sapling,
the soft plates of its bones denatured,
turned by the carpenter into barrel chests,
into the diaphragm of a man who has spent a lifetime laughing
high in the mountains at the abject beginnings of rivers.

The carpenter laughs in his hands;
you can see it balled there in blisters.
You can see that the splinters go into him
with alacrity, with the pleasure and rhythm of song.
And when he turns to you in the sawshed,
where you are a boy let loose for the first time with hammers,
and gets you to sand down the gunwales,
you take your biggest breaths;
you slip into the wood as a man shoves away from the shore.

## For a Nominal Form

In light that is meticulous,
having come between the hemlock limbs
and then between the beech,
it took some hours to take an aging hardwood down.

Wood is insufficient
to judge a length of time.
Look where the rings perplex as stains,
where the lines are pale and uncertain,
acknowledging a year that could have figured
other ways.

A rocking chair could be a piece
of something fallen from a clock.
It moves in its mechanics
like a metronome to signatures
of thinking in the floor boards.
The wood that makes the chair is intonation.
It is more than the time it took to grow.
It is not the rings that one thinks of,
but the length it had taken this to come to this.

## Natural Habitat

Like the rhododendron,
I too am startled by the late spring snow.
It is easy to simply put the boots away,
leave the ashes in the wood stove
as a kind of casual rib:
look, the fire has burned and its body can lie there,
I don't need to think of this.

But the rhododendron is not so brash,
its leaves emerge like umbrellas
opened just away from buildings,
as if to say I am uncertain,
my branch-work might be cursed,
the elbows of stove pipes
that could separate in the night.

Its flowers cluster together, looking
from a distance like one bald-faced bloom,
and the sudden snow today, like what foams
from a punched mouth.
The rhododendron is heavy in the yard
with the weight of having done nothing
to deserve this.

Still, it does not provoke the snow.
I go out on the driveway in my shorts,
even the tulips are steadfast and turgid,
their bulbs like smoothly knotted rope.
Somewhere in its vascular switches,
the rhododendron remembers the mountains,
the punishments descending
out of clear and faithful air.

## Sympathetic Nervous System

As though a way of knowing,
a killdeer comes down
upon the willow.

His plumage is out of the sky,
is an autonomic landing,
an unerring touch.

The willow is a head of long, wet hair
lifted straight from a basin,
each leaf a parallel stream.

When I think of my hands in your hair,
it is the involuntary smell of rain
on the husks of winter-scorched grass,

that moment in late spring
where the humidity makes the seeding poplars
into a procession of orthodox priests

waving their open lanterns of smoking clove.
What do you know? They ask.
What do you know about what you will do?

The killdeer knows that the mudflats are dry.
When it rains, the earthworms emerge;
their folds are the curves of a cerebellum

coming out of the water-tangled ground,
a head lifted far under the dirt,
standing in sympathy with flight.

## When at First the Doubt Appears

By the side of the road, staring at each other,
the horses are jackknives partially opened;
their angles are scrutiny, the sudden antagonism
of shoulders. The wind you watch in the fields
is a body fooling itself, hooves that beat
in your chest. A night of bedding down
and bedding down again.

When at first the doubt appears,
it is the opposite of language.
It is a pigeon torn apart on someone's lawn;
the landlord that takes too long
to remove the half that's left
ignoring the shredded linen of its feathers.
The next time someone speaks of birds,
it is the horse-like stare you give.

We stare now as the birches gain their leaves
and think of last fall
as they practiced their own deaths.
We cannot doubt so fearlessly;
our shoulders stiffen as the horses stand
in the field, the hay blows into our clothes
and its ears are a mess in the wool.

## The Distance Is Taciturn

Too often the ending is horizon,
is the maladroit of mountains,
the flat report of the sea.

The birds do not begin
and end in such an arrangement.
The clouds are not ascending thrones,

they tip themselves in curvatures,
as asymptotes, as bones
that do not touch us.

We watch as shorebirds leave the shore,
drop from what we see,
become as flat and final codas,

urgently. Things do not pass over us,
hold an even flight, but are rueful
as our voices angled outward, grave and falling.

# Rejoinder

To my astonishment,
a girl came out of the lilacs
and rode her bicycle
straight into a pond.
Her outstretched legs
were the lifted necks
of mallard ducks,
as they beaded and fled
in the kicked-up light.
Seeing this made me think of a woman
I had known as a child
who collected empty vessels
which she did not fill.
Any flowers she received as gifts
were given to me to plant in the lawn,
or dry on the spokes
of my bicycle wheels.
Often, I imagined her late at night
crouched near the lip of a pottery vase
listening to the bloom of azaleas,
the rustle of corn stalks,
trying to gather the nerve
to reach inside.
It was the way the mallards
froze at first
that made me think of her hand closing.

## The Podium

There is a need for this in winter.
The hemlocks take it upon themselves
where no other voice is possible.

They are Monsignors
arching in the gallery of the creek bed,
flinching to clear their throats.

The snow abides in the balconies,
is rapt in the branches as though the storm itself
were still occurring.

# Look at the Lake, Please

Loss is the weight of leaves
falling on leaves,
or the air displaced from lungs
when the heart swallows stones,
gulps them back, astonished.
It's feeling the weight of something
with a part of the body that you think
does not normally lift – the ventricles
open and close, they clench.
But blood is dragged through the body
like many-headed water that leaves
lift from the ground, through stems,
to give to the air.

Loss is the creak that all four chambers make
when the weight of her leaving slumps in.
But you lift yourself up by the blood
a hundred times a day.
As though the world were self-evident,
the frenzied birches on the shoreline
are filled with exasperated pumping.
Into you, the weight of breathing
floods wind that once smoked
over the low-hanging cloth of the lake.

## Eastern Hardwoods

By the beginning of November,
the forest is a cabinet of rifles.
Between the barrels,
your footsteps ricochet
and the way you've come
ticks blindly around you,
an engine that's stopped in the cold.

What has left comes again to leave:
your first dog, whose hips
became the softened middle
of waterlogged oaks,
wandering once more to these woods,
his head an Indian Summer,
a last, smoked thinking.

Her voice on the phone
says goodbye, strained
through the black cherry spines,
its timbre here again
in the wire, in the grey alloy
of being alone.

You ache for snow in the hardwoods,
for the way it proposes bones;
it takes some time to believe
that the last of the crows
do not simply explode
from the trees.

## Lake Filling in with Land

The spice bush
grows beside the hobble bush,
and among them
the star flower
believes above the bog.
We do not think
of eutrophy this way.
For the rest of the afternoon
we are uneasily watched
as we lie
on the part of the lake
that cannot catch
its breath.

## Driving Home

What rises out of the field
is a rusted truck;
the weather has worn its paint
a dark blue.
Of all the trucks you find in fields or bush
there are those, through rust and moss accretions,
that yield to an elemental colour,
divulging the base of their design.
At its end, the painted metal of the hood
recalls water that moved
the settlers in the valley,
its dark iris petals as a turgid fortune;
or yet recalls the sky above the farmhouse
aching with rain,
its blue cramp the impetus to move.

Children grow up making forts in the cab,
they jump on the seat cushion springs.
Mud comes over the axle and
goldenrod flicks through the frame.
Early mornings, deer sift down from the woods
lifting their rocking-chair heads in the mist.
The truck knows but one way to move;
even as it rusts, it points out of the valley,
blue in the face,
headlights cracked on corduroy roads.

## Sleep Begins in the Mouth

We've discussed this half-asleep;
our tongues like piled cottonwood
in the dry, open field.
It's hard to know how to give
yourself to someone.
It's the astonished snow
that returns in May as cherry blossoms;
how for weeks the branches had committed
to a brown indolence.
It's the baritone groan of river ice,
a decision without warning to disband,
to dash its bones.
When you let your eyes droop,
the air comes into you
like into a grassland deep in the neck.
Here the horses eat from your hand.
The lump in your throat is flowering grain.

# Part II
# Cordillera

# Part II
# Cordillera

## Cartographer

Without you,
I have taken to drawing maps
on the backs of photographs.
On the coast in a raincoat
your smile has been dented by a lake,
the fluting arms of rivers
have made your shoulders
look like the bark of birches.

In Saskatchewan the contours tightened,
cliffs gave way under your breastbone,
thin roads held gravely to your hips,
and pressing firmly, the sky became an overturned train
with its freight the black of clouded hills.

I have held back ponds with beaver dams,
even marked the dashes of higher seasons.
In a black and white series of us at Wye Marsh
the hair has blown into your eyes,
it is as if you see the choke of sticks between us,
the wetland that swells the other side.
Even then you sensed that my hand was unsteady
as it gathered your hair from behind.

## Composition

You are careful to match the grains,
collecting strewn branches after high winds.
You keep a record of revisions
to reassemble the woodwinds,
straighten out the pines,
place each of the gusts
in their original time.
One must be precise, like the blades of music
in the measures of leaves,
to fully enact such topography,
tune to the whip-poor-will,
and find a way to release
the genius of a hill.

## Before We Learned to Live in One Place

When skiers pass in diagonal stride,
they are skeptical crosses in the trees,
an alphabetic motion
that speaks interrogatives:
Is this the spot? Is this?
Their bodies mark ballots
for the sovereignty of glide.

Before we learned to live in one place
we expected much of motion.
If touched correctly,
a thicket would release its slowest rabbit,
or a meadow its tangled deer.
For this we searched the country
divining the nourishment of soft meat
in the bulwark of crossing the land.

The skier can't expect to know more
than one foot in front of the other;
it is feeling for the edge of the stairs
in the dark, the resolve
that all bets are off, that the railways
we leave are splintered.
If skiing is hunting and gathering
it is only because you ask
how to spring your own flight –
a discipline of wings, a form of planting.

## Reinforcing the Watershed

If it should ever come to pass
that this hillside returns to the river
and the pickerel
move into the cedars
lodging in the knotholes
and sunning on the stems,
or should the granite shelves
transform themselves into fantastic waves
fanning the graves of surprised farmhouses,
then let us retreat to a new shore,
where far enough above
the revolutions of water,
we will find fossils
still stiff in their mantles,
like Loyalists pointing seaward,
being driven into the back country.

## Believing the First Words You Hear

When the axe jams in the log
it is memory
reaching to pull you in.
Cherry is the easiest wood to split;
its grains are straight
paved roads.
Maple makes me think of you;
it grows branches as though
committing to entirely new trees.
I think of the axe handle
alive in my hands,
I think of the leaves.

## In Late Afternoon Sun You Are Water Seen from a Train Window

If it is the ocean that moves upon the beach
like the legs of wet dancers,
or into the inlets with the polish of pointed toes,
then, as the glaciers
turned back from here and weakened,
and as their seas withdrew,
why did we climb out upon the shoreline?

In water, the light is a waltz,
casting footsteps
on the sides of shallow salmon.
Animals the size of a single cell
open a circle for their food,
engaging the decorum of dance.
Even fish the shape of stones
move like folk ballads
in the mud.

We could have remained beneath the waves,
grown bodies made for jigging,
built cities out of shells.
And on days when the sun
filled the gallery, and the winds lifted
we could have slipped away
to the beach, been flat-footed on the rocks,
our positions salt-water pikes,
each move a tuck of swells.

## Erratics

Here, the water is several hounds
clapping on the rocks around us.
Dogs in place of lapping waves –
such substitutions often go unnoticed,
unconsidered where they are found.
Like the tower of a church
that becomes a chain of lakes
as its windows exchange in the sun,
one seldom sees the ascension,
the division that has come.
The sky that turns to a field of mares
and then to the flesh of a trout,
assumes its weight above us
as if by right, or consequence.
I have kept my eye to the surface
and to the lie of sand just beneath,
but still I cannot say when the movement took place
when exactly the water grew round
and folded upon the beach
as wind in a dress,
then into the feet of a hound.

## How We Look at Maps

In the living room, the bright skull of Africa
is pinned to the carpet with a piano stool.
The islands of the Far East
are hibiscus cuttings
spread out on the kitchen table,
the names of their cities
like the growth properties of stems:
Jakarta. Hanoi. The vigour of these.

When you lean on an elbow,
an atlas can be flipped through
with one hand.
There is always the page where London
is less than the width of a wrist
from the barbed shoulder of India,
hunching to push the Himalayas into China
as though they too had misused their empire.

And then outside, where the rain
has tipped its watershed into the driveway,
and dappled a shield of puddles,
Africa lifts its head, the stone grip of its jaw
in the fallen branches that float there.
India emerges where the car tires have dug.
The rain soaks you, it hangs hair
in your eyes like an unsettled cape.

## Knowing Where to Look

If it's a matter of learning to fly,
then who was the first student
to watch the breasts of leaves buoy
the limbs of prehistoric maples?
What quizzical avian saw the potential
of feathers in the hawking wings of elms?
If it's a matter of learning to love,
then do we build our nests in the trees
at our own peril? Do we risk a kind of flight
that teaches us to jump from the shoulders
of those whose roots have now busted
in through the bricks of our basements?

## Fortune

On the deck there is snow
and there is recent snow,
the flower pots are a set of back teeth.

Last night we watched the spring storm surge,
unfold its tent on the lawn, spread its clothes.
We drank orange juice with ice cubes.

The snow threw itself against the glass
like sluggish house flies at the end of the summer,
their bodies aiming dumbly.

With our drinks finished, we watched the weather
tend to the camp. It angered easily, not remembering
to fill its gusts, or push them all at once.

We thought it a good thing
we had forgotten to put the bulbs in the flower boxes.
The ice cubes cracked in the backs of our mouths.

## Into the Field

At the warmest part of the day
the tall grass soaks our pants,
determined that the rain in the night
should not go unnoticed, be like the desk
in the school room that is neat and empty,
the boy who sat there hardly mentioned by spring.

The water is upon us easily, modestly,
as though stuffed into our pockets
after a generous dinner with friends.
It moves through the fabric at first
as a spilled jar of beads, and then
as a chain of eutrophic lakes.

Once, the way the sun would smell to us
balled up in the hillocks of hay,
was as keen as the places yet to be cut,
maelstroms of grass bunched about the field
like a fierce temper, precariously held
to a pursed and golden steam.

But the water now that troubles our shins
serves only to make us limp,
belaboured by the weight of our clothes,
the unsettled bulk of our step,
like the boy who had at first for a day
come back in September.

## Falling and Falling Blues

Nothing falls down easily;
snow gets ripped in the pines.
I'm not very good at catching
your eye.

Deer bed down under apple trees;
I can see them open-mouthed.
I can't speak to you
this loud.

If I were a kind of tall grass
I'd string into your room;
I'd practice being a piano,
a loom.

In my descending stems,
I can only play caprice;
lie among the apple cores
with me.

## To Grand Manan Island

A pickup waits for the ferry. Its axle hangs
too far beneath its corrugated box,
it is a man whose jeans have slipped down
his narrow hips and stands slouching toward
the black and barnacled water at the edge of the pier.

The engine lurches as it raps on the planks to board:
a slung package of shingles, first to the knees
then to the shoulder and wearily up the ladder.
The axle clanks the raised step of the ramp
and limps into the hull with its greased trousers.

We wait by the lifeboats with our hands on our waists,
wondering if they will need to call deck hands
down to roll everything out when we get there.
The noises soften below us like the cuffs of pant legs
on a gangway, the ropes are loosened from shore.

## The First Time You Meet

At some point speed comes into you
taking up residence in the solar plexus,
its rhythm there like a toboggan.

It gives itself to be sculpted
in the sudden corners, the shifts
of weight, the way birds move on the ground,

their heads a gunfire of photographs.
There is no denouncing your heart
when it pounds downhill to her house

and your eyes are patched with snow.
Crash landings appear around you
as the discovery that gravity

spends the winters drinking,
its mittens slur snow down the neck of your coat,
your words taste of fish-tales and rust.

## Learning to Swim

I suggest that they might want
to swallow a bullfrog to help
getting in and past the weeds.

Quite beyond such monkey work,
the young girls are modest birches
holding their braids above the lake.

They refuse to laugh at me,
but cross their arms and hold
their bodies as firm and serious bandages.

The thin cough of an osprey breaks
above us, as if to say the way
to think of this is to be done with it and lunge.

The wind pushes the water into knots,
makes it white, the shine of bikes
knocked over in the sun.

The oily chains of seaweed kink and wave
their febrile tongues, and look hungry
for the wet scarves of pony tails.

The girls tiptoe onto the sand
with clenched and drumming steps,
their bathing suits are ensigns.

## Archipelago

You and I, as the tips of mountains,
slip into the sea like islands,
each conceiving differently
of water.
We touch along the thin glare
of an isthmus,
urging the tide into unclasped fans.
In the event of a storm,
we break open the weather
on the hard points
of our hunched spines.
But together, just below the surface,
as a pair of merging strands,
the migrations start
and the currents catch
on our misdirecting hands.

## Mapping in Seven Parts

I

There are tectonics
in the habits
of an oak.

In February, the steel light
grips through the boughs
like dishes covered in oatmeal.

The snow sits unswept
on the banister
of an uninviting stair.

You can hear its slow carboniferous
grind in each of the casts
the oak tree takes.

In the middle of the night
you think of roots
that must touch beneath the street.

II

There is something pitiable
in the play of light
on a dinner table set in the afternoon.

The cutlery glints in its cloudless
accomplishment, the embouchure
of wet loons.

In its own gymnastics,
the performance seems over-intent,
tactless and smug as stainless steel,

it is a garrulous surgery.
When the guests are finally seated
no one uses their hands,

or swallows without chewing.
Somewhere a hawk peels for a dive,
its body this thoughtful and whetted.

III

It is never dark methodically,
the overcast is bedclothes
worn under a pair of jeans.

At dusk the dimming acts
as though it cannot remember exactly
how to be effortless.

Sometimes the glowering light
is an overturned chest of scarves
and mittens fumbling in the hall.

When the only bulb in the room bursts,
the darkness is a single nectarine
balling in the bowl of your eye.

Around its candelabra,
the closet and dresser emerge like photographs
rolled where the edges were hot.

IV

Where one side of your parents' former house
has collapsed, the red scar is the shape
of the north shore of Prince Edward Island.

Before you were old enough
to easily fill a glass from the tap
you pulled your mineral limbs up the counter,

kicking the cupboard doors
in a clamber atop the escarpment,
its face an occasion of nesting peregrines.

The cold spoon of the faucet gripped your chin,
it coloured your cheeks
where the stream had slapped and run.

You remember the view of the harbour,
where the water is let into the inlet and kicks.
The shore is a vulnerable building.

V

It is the clear intelligence of snow drifts
at this temperature.
They shift on a hinge

as finely balanced as a morning
where a grosbeak stops at the window
and we do not let the dishes knock in the sink.

They are suddenly vertebrate,
an animal whose curvature
regales it.

When we talk of being satisfied,
we mean such an exodus,
a voluble walk in the parlance of horse tails.

I watch them form in the boneless,
hollow street,
I want them to stand against the windows.

VI

In some respects
our bodies inversely complement
the rain,

like building
a fire with wet wood.
I mean that we cannot occur

as rightly, the way the Hebrews
thought of God, a ripe melon
filled with water,

the way the leaves spark and fatten,
are the easy throats
of dipped paddles.

The rain smells in our hair of crushed fruit,
like a desecration
it smoulders.

VII

The elms are already petrified,
though they overdo it, perhaps,
on sunless afternoons

as strokes of stone lightning.
Looking up it is not difficult
to get turned around in the bark,

start to recognize where you may have been,
the crags tucked into the passes,
the packhorses stumbling.

The trunk is dirt that has been rifled through,
a premises hastily searched;
something is buried there, seized in its alps.

The animals know this before we do,
they jerk their bodies, reach the electric wires,
seeds trail from their mouths.

## The Return

We turn to maps of Eastern Europe
when we have been apart for too long,
grown unfamiliar with the bare arms
that have opened in the habits between us.
We speak of regions in Ukraine
where the soil must be a nest of blackbirds,
boisterous in the summer heat
thatching the sun like sheaves of wheat.

We understand the names of rivers
have been exchanged in the dark
on more looming nights than this.
To draw our fingers from Crimea to the Baltic,
and to linger for a moment on the steppes,
is to fill our chests with blackbirds and redress.

# Part III
# Standing Water

# Part III
# Standing Water

# The Question of Whether the Bread Was Noticed

A loaf of bread is hardening on the workbench
to a brick of white water,
a stilled froth of sockets.
An overturned canoe sits like a loosely rolled map;
it has been repaired in the garage during lunch.
The work was steady,
and the baking sat unnoticed,
sliced on a cutting board,
like a terraced grove of opened milkweeds.

The rock could not be seen from upstream,
the water moulded over its surface
like the shine that seeps and is dressed
on the skin of a burned finger.
The canvas split and a rib cracked,
the canoe was swung around like a plant
overburdened by its blossoms,
a heavy pod the moment before
its forceful hatch.

The bread was not eaten.
It ripened on the workbench to a single, cooling cut,
a thrust of the cataract held in place
by the clenched bark of its crust.
The repairs were made in the ribs
amid disagreement for sometime after
as to how a canoe stiffens
when one first steps in from the dock.

## In Terms Unfamiliar

It has been thirty years
since fire bared and bent across the hillside,
leaving a salt of black crows.
For a week in May, it has been said,
the sunsets turned away
into the lids of swollen eyes.

This spring, you and I
inhabit the upper limbs of maples,
climbing through the uncoiling shade.
We stand on the chest of the valley,
smelling the seeds,
watching the wind being made.

Perhaps it was our laughter,
or the slash of our bright clothes,
but unmistakable,
as if eager for flight,
a crow in a nearby mountain ash
flicked a glance of coal.

## In the Upper Reaches

The banjo player is at odds with his sound.
He picks quickly under the jack pines,
but the notes ascend and glut in the branches,
the music bulges, hangs differently than expected –
a kind of soothed melancholy,
a town that has burned and where things
have started to pick up again slowly.
He cannot explain how brisk
and folksy reels could come back to him
with the weight of having passed
through gutted parlours.
He pinches a cigarette in the strings
and re-tunes his banjo.

As children we would bat
the cones of the jack pine with sticks.
Their hard shells would drop
as though down a deep well
into the parched throat of the ravine.
We always understood that we could not
get them to break, that only the heat
would make their jackets split.
We thought of the neighbourhood razed,
the smoke still crouched in the gutters
and the ripened seeds of the jack pine,
cracking open like the clasps
on an instrument case.

## Among Branches

One afternoon I saw you
returning to the treetops
a bird's egg.

Perhaps I have been suspicious
of wood for too long,
without thinking,
betrayed the willows about me,
said that their leaves were leathery.

But I have lived with the boreal at my back,
with disappearing rivers
raked by trees
until they've been shredded
and hung about the land
in moist skins.

I have encouraged the birds to leave,
lifted shrill speech in the brush,
acted the alarm of the warbler,
and posed as a kestrel
above the thin china of a nuthatch young.

And yet you trust the treetops
as you walk beneath them,
place the new bird among the branches
as though you had comfortably unravelled the riddle,
seen the migration in a single stem,
the deep and sluggish oceans
that crept upon us like wet clothes.

I watch as you leave
and cannot help but think of the rivers
making a final stand in these woods,
and offering, as you offered,
the sound of clear throats
to the canopy,
the promise of flight
to the back of the world.

## Pressed Against the Gunwales

As though the sides of weakened boats,
we can't keep the raspberries
from thrusting up between us.
We are as Ditchburns
overturned behind the house.
The planking has grown grey and blue
as lips too long in the bay,
the ribs shift in their sleeves
and don't brace,
like the hold of cottongrass
on a wet, exposed cliff.

In places where the rain has come straight in,
the wood has turned black
and has crept like farmland
back into the spaces that have been still.
Underneath, the grass has died,
and the ferns are spilled salamanders
finding nothing beneath us
but the dry language of stacked bricks.

Only the raspberries have prospered,
dragging the length of their stems
like astonished, dislocated jaws through the woodwork.
The berries bead on our hulls;
they are the drops that don't open,
the surf that doesn't yield to the prow,
the water that can't leave a whisper,
but remains in the mid-air of an open mouth
dangling above overturned bodies
like arteries full and unable to pulse.

## Corpus Callosum

From some angles
these trees make perfect sense.

They don't crowd
the electric wires,
or curl into the foundation
like bitter, wooden frosts.

They don't threaten to splinter
into climbing children,
or catch in the throat
of a startled mother.

When all of the leaves
have been stripped,
the upper branches
snap their wings,
and like one side of a brain,
peer endlessly through
the sense of things.

## We Tried to Keep from Slipping

Skating out of doors
is like recognizing a duplicity in rhythm.
The lake is a bottle
beneath the blade.
It is the black column
of a pipe organ
where the air has stretched
through a cleft,
its hard anchor of gneiss.

But out in the middle of the lake,
where the surface creaks,
we could be the weight of guests
shown into a sitting room,
our conversation like sunlight
off the bright backs of boathouses,
the white planks in the flooring beneath us,
as the thought of Strauss
in the syllables of our feet.

During the course of our skate
to the island,
the bedrock gripped its glaring pipes,
the parlour clicked to our beat,
but the ice remained uncertain for us,
a band that had not yet played,
that had altered its company,
and handed its sheet music aside.

## Celestial Mechanics

The stars clatter
on cold nights.

We start again
to the window.

## Interpellation

What is disappointing about the river
is that even where it narrows to slip
over the thin shelf of rocks and slacken
in the calm, bulged bay at the bottom,
it does not seem to be listening.
Even now the stiff groan of the poplars,
the killdeers that flick their songs like bottle caps
that skip among the uneven boulders,
pay some attention to each other,
announce their cacophony as one.
But the river heaves its static down
in overzealous gulps, in the stridency
of a boy who chews his food open-mouthed,
a child perpetually on the verge
of walking, that doesn't know to stand
and move its feet, only that a lower place
will bear its weight and so the body simply falls.
There is no conversation to be had,
no rational coming to terms.
There is only the chance of a well-placed surprise,
of a face, or a gesture that grabs its attention,
of a kindness, perhaps, to which it might be
inclined to pause and come crawling back up.

## A Kind of Vertigo

Ever since the mine shaft imploded,
he has remained above ground.
Friends have moved things from the basement
so that he doesn't have to go down.
They have taken the stairs off the path to the beach,
and filled in the garden with clay;
should he reach down for these things,
to sink his hands out of habit,
nothing would give way.
The trees have become black retina,
and a complex of knotted nerves.
He is convinced that the dirt flinches and climbs
through each of the branching curves;
he has kept to ladders in the yard
to stay above their sifting glance,
carefully pruning where he can.
The pipes have been excavated,
and the earth pulled away from the well,
but even still, the water seems suspicious to him.
He has smelted the gold from his rings
and hurled it out to the bay,
but he doesn't move around much now:
in a moment of level-sea and clear-cape, he cut off his feet,
nothing could condone the company they keep.

## The One Virtuous Act of the Dictator

The crow sat in the poplar like a black boot.
He was, at first glimpse, a prank,
the remnants of an unruly evening
beside the only rail lines in town.

One of the laces dangled from his beak,
a stick that he had clipped and untied.
When the crow stretched his neck,
he was a boot that reached to the knees.

From the wooden balustrade
he cast his decoration,
it hurried through the branches
in the slapping of its own applause.

When I caught the stick, the crow
quit the tower, his body an adamant march
beyond these houses, back to his bunker
having simply made the trains run on time.

## When Light Lies Thirty Feet Across

We are the temper two rivers
assume together in the fall,
joining at even temperatures
and sweetened by the blush of sugars
from sodden leaves. We swell upon
the chutes as filling feathers.

Above the river at sunset,
splashing themselves across a sky
of broken cloud, the birds are
shallow water over rock.
For us the spangle of rapids
is the sound of breaking camp.

With canoes we play in birches
that are strung along the shore,
as open hands, setting bullfrogs
from the fingers with our paddling.
Downstream we are blue herons
in the light before lifting.

## Travel

From above the docks,
she responds to the daylight
by opening a window to hang the sheets.

The weather fills them like throbbing fish,
she retreats at their ungainly language;
such bodies come upon her in this place.

She knows already,
that the wind is not just near her,
that the way of it is palimpsest.

She thinks herself a country,
where the sky has broken through,
the sounds of its fins crest in her throat,

turning even the silence awash.
Her mind is unrehearsed,
it is close to her and forceful.

## I Tell You This Is What I Do Not Tell You

You ask me from the hallway:
what are the things that I see from windows
and do not think to tell you?
The question makes me think of the river
and the blades of young girls diving
from the roofs of boathouses.
At the moment when their bodies
meet the water, they are cattails,
stippled in the shoreline with rills.
They are a tipped tray of after-dinner drinks,
when the music has turned buxom
and has filled to the size of the house, and out
through the open windows to the water.
They do not see me as they climb back up
to the boathouse,
their bathing suits like leaves pressed
to the wet stems of their waists.
I tell you that the river is a kind of light.
It soaks the stratus of certain afternoons,
and then affords a murky gloom,
lighting the underside of docks and cedars,
lingering in the wet hair of swimmers.
I tell you this is what I do not tell you,
and I close the door to the room.

## In Between Points of View

The night he drives into the country,
the windows are down,
the air smells of guitars.
It's the lacquered spruce and rosewood
that flood into the car,
he thinks of children bathing naked
in a river with Labs. The smell is hair,
or wood that has been next to hair.
They move their bright bodies
into the sound box, like wet rocks
he once put in to give the jig
a steeper stomp.

He stops the engine,
shuts the lights, unfolds his body from the car
as though getting a drink, taking the guitar
from his knee for a moment.
The air is as thick as a folk song
written on a raft in a river
after a dinner of dark bread.
He does not leave without checking the ditch
to see where the dog dove.

# Calling in the Dogs

He doubted as a child
when the dogs needed to be called for dinner.
Would this be the day they would not come,
be too far into the caged acoustic of grass?
He curled his voice to its fullest barrel
hoping to reach the fence post at least,
but if the humidity of dusk did not tear it,
then the loping blades of the corn husks
or the rake of the hay field beyond
would leave it in the undergrowth
like a sand of unopened seeds.

The dogs would eventually arrive.
Sometimes cracking into the house
like the heated shells of chestnuts,
or a sudden volley of muskets,
the sound of their paws on the pine,
a rowdy quarrel of revellers.
After dinner they would come
to lay their heads on his knees.
He never knew if they had heard him,
but would pick the seeds
from the snag of their coats
and save them in a bowl by the bed,
trying to hear if his voice had broken.

## Great Slave Lake Disclosure

The problem with us is the east arm
of Great Slave Lake. For too long
we have been as perfunctory as riverbanks,
certain of the lower places, the mud
that creeps like chinking into joints between the stones.
Red-throated loons have lately pushed
into our conversations with the authority
of boulders collared with gneiss.
When it's been weeks since we've spoken,
from innumerable islands we hear
the pitch of flightless black spruce.

The water in the arm is confused with rocks,
a fever of bays and peninsulas that long ago
lost any memory of shoreline, of Precambria,
a homeland where things had not yet cooled.
The arm is something started and then stopped.
An agriculture of cold, of growing out of touch
and back upon itself like bones that lose direction
after breaking, it is thinking that is poorly drained,
a mess of undecided lakes, granite and trees
half soaked, our plans, retreating pike
in unlocked schools.

## The Shifting Weight of Staying

There is no walkway around the house.
To build a retaining wall in the back yard
the workers must carry the railway ties
through the living room.
Two men to each tie,
holding their necks and shoulders in
between the bookcase and the clock,
as though discriminate, overbearing collectors
unimpressed by the commonplace.
They look straight ahead as they proceed,
the way cold slumps into the house through an open door,
settling into the room like porcelain.
The men move about in columns,
shifting their bodies in a cool allowance
for the knotted boil of pine in the coffee table,
or the bolts of daffodils
waving their grooves into the hallway.
They lift the ties above the crook of the chesterfield
and out to the back deck.
With the weight of them gone,
curious and furtive drafts resume
climbing and cupping in the hollows
of the room, revealing the unlikely leak of things.
The men return again empty-handed,
looking only at the creosote that is on them,
in the hair of their arms like a sweep of birches
that has burned in very little wind.
As they walk back through the living room,
they step on the pages of newspaper
that have been laid out for their boots.

## Concerning a Sudden Departure

From his seat,
a man presses the white belly
of his palms
against the train window.
His eyes pour past the station
beyond the dark ditch of the river.

He must be able to see the town
over the trees, the plumb bobs
of the swing-sets in the school yard,
their lurking buffoonery of steel and chain,
like an opened box of tackle
from where he looks.

As the wheels start to turn,
his hands are muskellunge
flinching for a moment against the reel.
From the angle of the platform,
a reflection of the sky bullies into its place
over the still pool of windows.

Perhaps he saw the rain coming,
hanging its mosquito net across the hill,
glimpsed the first far off chimney
spreading its smoke a bit too wide,
held his hands against the glass
as though all of it had refused to move.

Splintered clouds begin to bloat
as they lie across the cars
like the decomposing edge
of a mildewed fishing jacket.
The drops fall lightly on the tracks,
at first as shining crescent hooks.

# Fort Smith Fire Brigade

The ravens are as large and as loud as babies.
They are public tantrums
for food that has dropped in the dirt.
In the town parks, on the hydrants,
they are wood leftover
from a catastrophic fire, a black that gulps
daylight and holds it like a rain barrel,
a locked and scorched water.
They are ambassadors from the other side
of what-has-burned, laughter
that reverberates at the end of language,
rises up, its feathers of thinking smoke.
They treat the things we build
as furniture; the gas pumps,
the stop signs are slouching galleries,
are the relaxed mess of a building
they know they can leave.
A raven is the child that leaps into your throat
when branches have fallen in the street.
It is the part of you that grows younger
when first you realize at night
how well the dark takes up residence
among the open, leafless stars.

## Beetroot

The ore of her thinking
is red,
like the flush from standing
too quickly
at the end of a day of gardening.
Her fingers are asparagus stalks,
stubbed and coiled cucumbers,
thick from years of having carried the charge
of her burly, grandmotherly care,
the pots of turnip
that needed lugging to the kitchen.
She digs her hands in the soil,
abstracts the weeds
with the informality of a doctor
who has decorated a lifetime
in the service of a single organ.
When she works, the rose of her kerchief
covers her hair.
She wipes her forearm against it to rest,
the dirt has dried in the folds
and falls away crisply
like heels of rye that have been opened
over borscht.

## The Part of the Flag Nearest the Staff

Near the beach the flags
are rasping,
the sultry air a ruckus
lurched in the tin hot dog stands,
in the umbrellas
like several rounds of drinking.
A young waitress washes nervously
between the tables, a whitecap cresting
as her apron barrels and snaps.
She cannot close a parasol
that has blown its knuckles
upward and locked like a webbed claw.
Someone has thrown a crust in its palm,
the gulls lose patience above her.

She raises her arms and looks
down on the beach,
the surf is spilling its kettle,
jellyfish parachute out of the steam.
The wind coughs up from the seashore,
and she wants to loosen her apron,
but her fingers are rushing,
her knuckles are stiff, they lock
in the midst of untying.
She needs to calm down
for a moment and sits.
Above her the flags are sheet metal
lifted and thrown to the beach.

## Introducing or Being Introduced

The clouds stand as boxcars,
the domains of a dark magnet,
the mortar between the sky
and water.
She can see them thinking past the rails,
past the metal castings lying in the yards,
to a polished column of pianos
assembling in their concert keys.
I tell her no. They are boxcars,
empty and returning to the coast.

I lift our hands to touch the rusted doors,
she spreads her fingers to receive them,
we smell the grain, the livestock loaded
from the planks of small town stations,
and move between the flatbeds,
the open-topped sawdust bins.
She keeps her eyes closed,
directing her hands in the air
as though conducting freight to the side.
Her body tightens to the curve of the whistle
that moans down on us
like the end of a shift,
or a piano tuned in our building.

# Acknowledgements

Thanks are due to the following publications where some of these poems first appeared: *The Fiddlehead*, *The Malahat Review*, *The Antigonish Review*, *Grain*, *Pottersfield Portfolio*, *The New Brunswick Telegraph Journal*, and *Bywords*. Several of these poems were previously broadcast on Atlantic CBC Radio. "Archipelago" first appeared in *Stroll of Poets: The 2001 Anthology*. "Falling and Falling Blues" first appeared in *Why I Sing The Blues*, edited by Jan Zwicky and Brad Cran, Smoking Lung Press, 2001.

Many thanks for feedback, friendship, and encouragement to: Seymour Mayne, Ryan Suter, Joseph Dunn and the Ottawa U. Poetry Group, Sue Sinclair, Marla Becking, Eric Hill, David Seymour, Shane Rhodes, Eric Miller, Lynn Davies and the Ice House Poetry Collective in Fredericton.

Thanks to St. Peter's College and the "Conversation and Silence" group.

Special thanks to Andy Weaver for many provocative discussions and to Jennifer Chambers for close reading, insight, and guidance. I wish to thank Ron Stevens and Wayland Drew for early encouragement and for helping me in ways that I am still realizing. I am grateful to Ross Leckie for his generosity and invaluable assistance at every stage of this book.

I thank my editor, Marnie Parsons, for her keen poetic attention, for her enthusiasm, and for making this book come together. Thanks to all the wonderful people at Brick.

"The Distance is Taciturn" is for Jan Olesen.
"When Light Lies Thirty Feet Across" is for my parents.
"Beetroot" is for my late grandmother, Annie Mykitko.

## Biography

Adam Dickinson was born in Bracebridge, Ontario, where he
grew up around the Muskoka Lakes. His poems and reviews
have appeared in a number of Canadian literary journals. The
collection that became this book won the 1999 Alfred G. Bailey
Prize for the best unpublished poetry manuscript from the
Writers' Federation of New Brunswick. He lives in Edmonton
where he is a Ph.D. student at the University of Alberta and a
co-editor of *The Olive* journal and reading series.

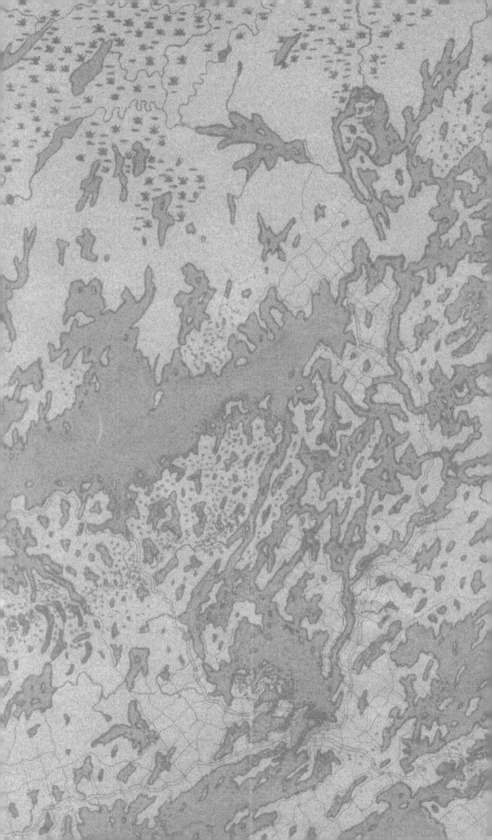